Fight Within

Dr. Himanshi Raheja

BookLeaf Publishing

India | USA | UK

Presentation by *BookLeaf Publishing*

Web: www.bookleafpub.com

E-mail: info@bookleafpub.com

ISBN: 9789360948726

First edition 2024

Dedication

For GaurNitai

My whole life depends on their mercy, and I dedicate all my work to Gaur Nitai. They are the source of all my strength.

Acknowledgment.

First and foremost, I thank God for giving me
such beautiful dream and then helping me to
fulfill it. I thank my husband who took care of
all the minor details just for this book to look
good. He has been my inspiration throughout.
My parents, my sisters and all my family who
encouraged me in every decision I took. My
brothers, who I want to make proud at every step
of my life. Last but not the least my friends who
made sure I enjoy all my journeys. Thank you
all for being in my life. You are a blessing.

God be the Witness

Quiet in my mind and in my heart
Closed my eyes and feeling apart.
Shake me up and wake me up
Before I fall take me up.
I wait and wonder what I left
Happy and sad, nothing I felt.
Collecting myself again along with my soul
Making a chance I will give it a call.
I know I will tumble
A slight I may fumble.
But to my destination I proceed
God be the witness as I succeed
God be the witness as I succeed.

#Fightwithin

Be a Queen

We try and we fail
We practice, we master

And then we prevail.
Fall and rise
Learn and be wise.
When distractions we curtail
Great success we hail.
If chance none taken
And the soul is not shaken
Victory can't be tasted
Spirit all wasted.
So gather the courage
Work harder.
Stop at nothing
Prepare your armour.
Win win you get
Win win you dream.
Build your kingdom
And be a Queen.

#Fightwithin

Never got Noticed

Ain't me a phoenix when it comes to living?
I accept, get defeated but never stop believing
I gave it all, I made it all
But hardly was I noticed.
I was told it's my duty and no reward should it
consist.
One step a day, I told this to myself.
It's a lonely journey, I am getting no help.
It was paining but I stopped complaining.
I guess I was just too tired of explaining.
But then I found a ray of light.
I wasn't sure as it wasn't much bright.
But the chance I took and moved towards.

It was the strength I built which literally was an
award.
It's okay if I get no appreciation from the world.
I have a proud face even if a bit wrinkled.
I know I gave my best
And I know, God will take care of the rest.

#Fightwithin

I am not Special

I stepped out into the world
But was suddenly pulled inside
I had desire of being the first
But I was still standing behind
Least were my chances I was told
Nothing special in me that I hold
The world is full of passion
And flaunting is now the fashion
I can't fight, I was strongly informed
And even if I try I will be wronged.

I believed them for a while
I closed the door with a smile.

But one day.

I sat at the window from dusk to dawn
And with the ray of light I was newly born.
It's not the competition that I require
But just have to polish what I acquire.
Life is not the war that needs a victory
It's a simple formula there is no mystery.
Just be you and the explore the sky
With your own wings you learn to fly.
And even if you fall and break your wing
Worry not just walk and in happiness you sing.
Move ahead everyday till the day you die
And live in peace before the final goodbye.

#Fightwithin

I stood Again

Empty rooms and old ceilings
Warm winds and deserted feelings
A window and a chair
Both shining in despair.
A road in my sight
And a vision in my mind
Sitting all alone
Escaping all the noise.
Building up my thoughts
And giving them no voice
Exhausted distorted I toss

I stood again.. again I rose…
I stood again.. again I rose.

#Fightwithin

Dying Dream

It was an empty home
Closed for ages I guess.
Dust and dirt all around
There wasn't any life's mess.
Though a dying essence of life was there
But cracks in the walls were widened.
Someone tried to live in I hope
But efforts were failed and saddened.
I can see the stains of some crushed flowers.
They were black and odourless
Some warmth was felt but fragile.
Suddenly then I saw a box
Which felt hopelessly alive.
The box was so rusty, hard to open
It was jammed and so stubborn

With all the strength I tried
I opened the box and I cried.
It was my dream sitting in my heart
All lonely and in despair.
Which was once my crucial part
I left it alone for life to happen.
But let me now carry it again
Let me now burn my lantern.
Let me give my dream a breath
And let me make it live till death.

#Fightwithin

Mirror

I am made up of mirror
I show less but more I bear.
I am little fragile but firm
Yes, little delicate yet stubborn.
Even into pieces I remain the same
Never lose my identity
I Never lose my flame.
Put me in the sun
And I will burn the ground.
Put me in the rains

And I will be more profound.
Dirty me with your hands
But I will still reflect a ray.
Block me all you can.
But I will still find a way.
As Mirror I am
And as Mirror I stay.

#Fightwithin

You Left

Mornings were all empty
Then I gave chance to the nights.
Still couldn't find peace
Dimming off were the lights.
I asked you not to leave me in the dark; that I
fear being alone.
You will leave me, I had an idea
I knew you are made of stone
I begged you, I prayed and cried
But you heard nothing
You left and little of me died.

Today, I stand and look back as I see
Not a day, a month, but years have passed and
you never returned.
All I hope is for the night to come back and give
no option of leaving
But darker it has grown
Covered with all the dusks till today's dawn.

#Fightwithin

Grace I talk

No, it's not all about you but me too.
I ask for, I crave for, and I die for you.
But no it's not all about you.
This is just a paradox I am trapped in
Hustling and fighting, I will take the win.
I stood apart just for once

So astounded I stand as I look more beautiful on
my own.
Concealed and covered behind you
Never imagined such elegant was my body.
So refined was my shape, so blooming was my
age.
A woman with a touch of girlhood that was not
dead yet
With all my dignity and head high I walk.
Fortitude I wear and grace I talk.
I know now I needed myself not you
Because no, it was never about you.

#Fightwithin

We got Married

I was standing in the crowd
And everything was just so loud
I wanted to disappear
I had big social fear
I wast lost in that noise
I was begging for silence, no voice.
Then you came from nowhere
And you held me so near
You were so calm and quiet
Only you were in my sight.
You saw me in pain and took me away

You fought the world and made me a way.
I knew that very moment you were the one
After everything I lost it's you that I won.
I was the happiest you filled my heart
I was ready for my new life to start.
With all the joy I accepted you mine
It was the time for my stars to shine.
But suddenly something was shaking me up
To the reality, someone was waking me up.
You were different, nothing was the same
You felt apart and we lost that flame.
We thought we loved each other
But all our feelings were buried.
Nothing wrong really happened.
We just got married.
We just got married.

#Fightwithin

It will change

You love, you hate or you just don't care
But you got what you got, change it if you dare.
Your words didn't get the voice
They were all trapped in your mind.
The rage resided in your heart
But you were taught to be kind.

Mortified soul you carried throughout
But the outer self was all glittering.
You prayed for everything you lack
But faith inside was a little flickering.

When you succumbed to despair
It was impossibly tough to again repair.

But as says the rule—nothing is constant.
Hold on it will change.
Just not that instant.

#Fightwithin

O Candle

O candle you burn, you burn so deep.
You stand so high and what destiny you meet.
You are all so white inside and out.
You let your beloved ignite you without a doubt.
You diminish your body but enlightened you
stay.
You fight the dark and keep making a way.
Tell me O candle don't you feel bad.
You give away yourself, don't you feel sad?
What gives you strength to keep this flame?
You shine so beautifully, what is your aim?
Tell me your secret, how are you so humble
How do you save yourself before you all
crumble?
Tell me what made you so resilient that you fear
nothing?

How to be a candle? Please tell me a little
something.
I want to glow like you and still never cry
I want to live like you before I die.

#Fightwithin

My Kitchen

I have a home inside my home
People call it kitchen.
First I didn't know the place
I got married and saw its real face.
Now I know why my mother decorated it so
well.
It's a safe haven for one who is no longer a girl.
I cook here for my child so that he remains
healthy.
I cook here for my family so that they remain
wealthy.
Daily in the morning I stand there for a while.
I make myself tea with an invisible smile.
This place has seen me from breaking inside.
But the walls here always stood by my side.
It never gets tired and exhausted
No matter how long I stay here.
It talks me out of my sadness

Rather holds me more near
I have shared my joy with my stove, glass and
plates
It always gives me back the same happiness
without any hate.
I may sound so simple talking about my kitchen
But it's not just a place but an escape
It's a portal to another world, which keeps me
safe.

Salvation of a River

I came across a river
But it wasn't flowing.
I asked what happened.
No life you are showing.
She came little near
And said she wanted to disappear
So hurt she sounded.
I looked where she was wounded.
I asked her what was it that she wished
She told me—
 "I am on a leash...
To be born here wasn't the choice I made.
If I get a chance I am ready to trade.

One life we get, everyone says,
Pain is more and forever it stays.
I want to flow but I am so much burdened
There are so many lives in me
And I can't leave them abandoned.
I want to run towards the ocean
And fulfil my ultimate destiny
I am trying to hold everything together
But slowly losing my sanity.
Take everything from me, I just ask freedom
I am deeply tangled that you cannot fathom
I want to move in peace without any obligation.
Let me reach my aim.
Let me have my salvation."

#Fightwithin

I played my Share

And the wind wasn't blowing
Sun went down
All voices were drowned.
Numb, desensitised, frozen and deprived I stand.
Staying apart from every human feeling.
No glories, no fame.
Neither a stigma, nor any shame.
I woke up, I saw
It wasn't my body...it wasn't me.
No skin to touch.
No pain to feel.

It was not my world I could see.
Abandoned was I and left free.
I closed my eyes and got lost in a flare.
I was gone forever.
I have played my share…
I have played my share.

#Fightwithin

God is the Answer

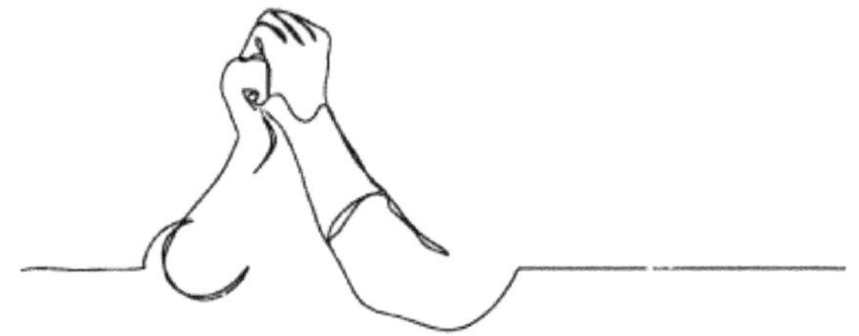

Sometimes the answer is silence
Be quiet and bear
Bear what you got, bear what you suffer
But just be quiet.
Complete silence.
Days will be hard, time may not pass.
You may feel totally dejected.
Your ideas may get frequently rejected.
But just be quiet and let it go.
Say nothing, just watch the show.
The world may blame you for everything.

In your heart, you may feel a sting.
You will be called a coward
And good for nothing.
But just stay silent, speak nothing.
And if one day this gets unbearable
Close your eyes and talk to your God.
Tell him to help you as you are unable.
Tell him to hold your hand and he will.
Because he listens to everything you say.
You will get your way.
God is the answer, come what may.

#Fightwithin

Young Girl

I knew nothing but love
I was definitely a young girl.
Fantasy is what I wished, hoped and lived.
I had my own little world.
I felt too valiant that I will win every war.
I kept going through bushes worrying no scar
I knew less but expressed more.

Everything I felt I just wanted to explore.
I had big dreams and I believed in them all.
I felt in my heart that I rule the world.
It was a beautiful age
There were no doubts.
I felt like flying on the ninth cloud.
I never wanted for those days to be over
But life has its own plans
No matter how much you wish
Destiny is written for every man.
But I still hope to be happy someday
That I will live again as a young girl.
I am lost now but I will be out of this swirl
I will fulfil all my fantasies one day
Just a few karma debts are left to pay.

#Fightwithin

Corona

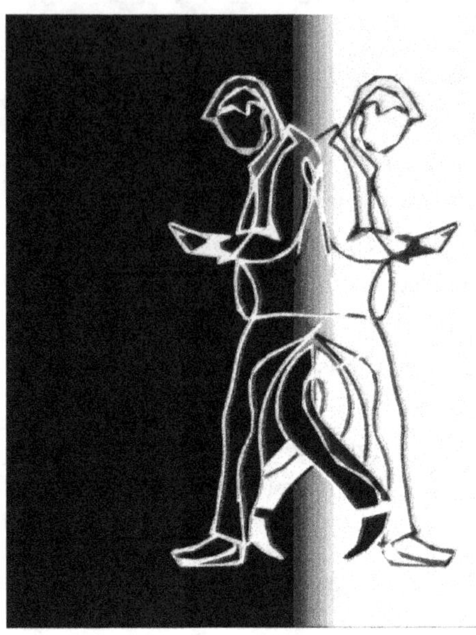

When the roads were full
And the shops were alive
News were flashing all over
That too live.
Humans have screwed big time
Now it's time to hide.
Silence spread in minutes
Nothing seemed fine.
Internet took over
Whole world was online.

Reality was virtual
And the truth was blind.
All the karma we did
Was now hitting us back.
We were closed in chambers.
Some were buried in the sac.
How come we got so in trouble
Why were we in a pathetic bubble?
Now when the terror has resided
Good path now should be decided.
Learn a lesson which nature taught you
Look where this recklessness brought you.
Step back and now turn for good.
Do whatever you should
Ignorance can not always be bliss.
If given a chance do not just miss.

#Fightwithin

My decisions

I don't know If I am doing it all right.
I just have a vision in my sight.
I am not aware of the paths to walk
I have no one to listen to, no one to talk.
I am just taking a leap of faith and trusting the time.
I am believing in God, if not sooner, one day I will shine.
I have hidden it all from everyone I see.
I know they will stop me from being me.
It's okay if I fail and do not succeed

Atleast I tried and that's all I need.
I want to take my decisions and live through
them all.
I will not regret if I reap what I saw.
Praying only to the God to hold my hand
And I will not fall if by my side you stand.

#Fightwithin

Closed gates

Do not now enter my world.
That you are no more allowed.
You failed all the chances you got
Now you better just stand out.
I believed in you with all that I have
I opened my heart in whatever way I can.
I exposed my truth and all the strength
I shared my emotions in full length.
But all you did was make me feel odd.
All my weaknesses were used as a sword.

But that's okay, I have learnt a lesson.
I got my answer without any question.
Now I know I have to work alone.
I will make my ways all on my own.
I have the courage to climb the mountain.
And I can do that alone, that's certain.
You were not all wrong that I am naive
You made me realise how to survive.
Now you stand out and just watch the show.
You played your part...
now see how far and high I go.

#Fightwithin